Miss Little's Gift

W9-DAS-487

Miss Little's Gift

DOUGLAS WOOD

illustrated by JIM BURKE

CANDLEWICK PRESS

eading was only one of my problems in the second grade at Longfellow Elementary School. I was the youngest student in Miss Little's class. I was the smallest. I was the newest — my family had just moved to Iowa from Kentucky — and I didn't have any friends. I also had a southern accent, and because of it, the other kids said I "talked funny."

"Try again, Douglas," said Miss Little as I struggled with the book in front of me. "See if you can sound that word out. Go ahead. . . ."

I tried again. Hard. Sort of . . .

Reading was no fun at all. The words and letters just sat there on the page — lines and blobs and squiggles that didn't mean anything. Well, they meant one thing. They meant that here I was again, the only student in Miss Little's second-grade class staying after school. Practicing reading.

I didn't like school. I didn't like sitting still. I didn't like reading. And I *didn't* like Miss Little.

I tried again. "Sha-sha-sha*dow.*"

"Good, Douglas. Now go on."

Miss Little turned around from cleaning the blackboard and looked at me. I went on.

"Spiders sailing their webs ag-against a g-gen . . ."

I was stuck again. "I can't do this, Miss Little," I said. "I'm never going to learn how to read."

"Oh, yes, you are, Douglas. You're going to become a *good* reader. We're going to do it together, you and I, even if you have to stay after school every day."

That was exactly what I was afraid of!

Staying after school had to be one of the world's all-time *worst* ideas. I had already stayed after school for getting into tussles on the playground, for talking when I wasn't supposed to, and for pulling Joan Brodie's ponytail.

But to stay after school almost *every* day, to practice reading with Miss Little? Rats!

Miss Little had seventeen students. And there was no student teacher or tutor around. If I was going to get extra help, I'd have to stay after school.

Miss Little had said that she saw something in me, and she was determined that I would learn how to read. Whatever she saw, I wished she hadn't seen it. Now look where I was — staying after school instead of outside throwing a football or catching a baseball.

I hated being cooped up indoors. I hated sitting still. My desk felt like a jail. I couldn't wait for summer, when I could be . . .

"Douglas." Miss Little's voice, firm but gentle, called me back to the classroom with its blackboards and its old tile floor. Back to my desk with its squeaky lid. Back to the book in front of me, with its squiggles and lines and dots.

Miss Little had finished grading papers and cleaning blackboards, and now she was standing right over me, pointing at the page.

"Why don't you start here?" she suggested, and I began once more.

"Against a g-g-"

"It's 'juh'—like *jar*, Douglas," she said.

"A juh-jen-jen-tell—gentle! A gentle wind," I read.

"Good, Douglas."

We went on.

I liked the pictures in the book. It was about an island, and the pictures showed blue sky and blue sea, green trees and rocky shores and fish, all things that I knew about and liked.

I knew about them because every summer my grandad took the whole family to a lake called Kabetogama, in Minnesota's north woods. It was a big name, Kabetogama, but I could say it. I could even *read* it, because I loved it so much.

At Kabetogama there were *many* islands — and gulls and loons, bear and deer and moose in the forest, rocks and trees and caves and secret places to be explored. And, of course, a great big lake full of fish just waiting for my grandad and me to catch them.

And we had a favorite island there, too. A place where once a very big fish had been caught. The previous summer we had had a picnic there, and I had caught a big old turtle in a net. I kept it for a week, and it was the neatest pet I'd ever had. But when it came time to go home, Grandad and I had decided to let it go, because it belonged in Kabetogama.

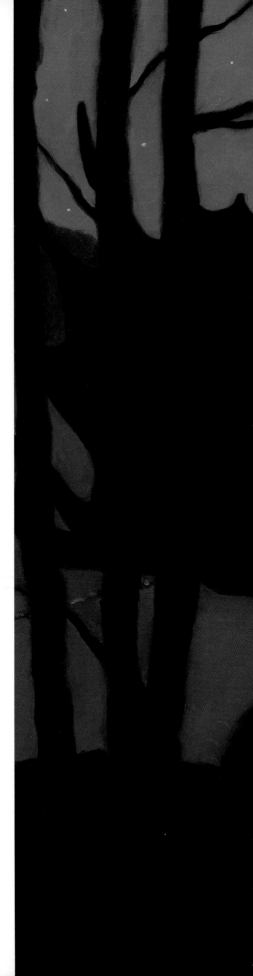

Now, as Miss Little stood beside me, I began to feel more interested in this book, *The Little Island,* and wondered what would happen next. I wondered what the words would tell me about the Little Island, because the pictures didn't show everything.

There were *lob-sters* hiding under sea *ledg-es.* I didn't know about lobsters, but they seemed kind of like the crayfish my grandad had shown me at Kabetogama. There were seals that came down from the north to raise their babies on the Little Island. There were gulls laying eggs and wild *str-straw-straw-ber-ries* just ripe for picking. I knew how to find them.

Then came the best part. A boat came to the island carrying some people on a picnic! I didn't like the way that word *picnic* was spelled. It ought to be *pik-nik*—anybody could see that. But I figured it out and went on. I wanted to know what was going to happen on the *pik-nik* on the Little Island.

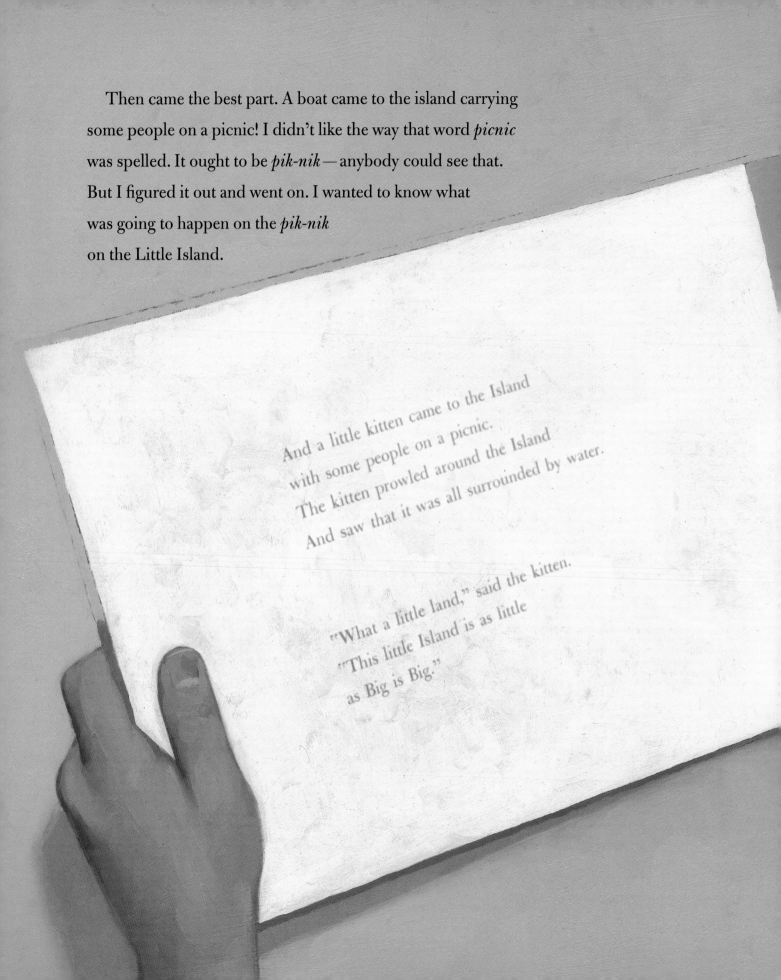

And a little kitten came to the Island
with some people on a picnic.
The kitten prowled around the Island
And saw that it was all surrounded by water.

"What a little land," said the kitten.
"This little Island is as little
as Big is Big."

A little cat came to the island with the people. The cat explored the island, just as I explored Kabetogama. He found dark, secret places and met fish and animals and learned secret things.

I could imagine all the secret things he found and how excited he was to discover them.

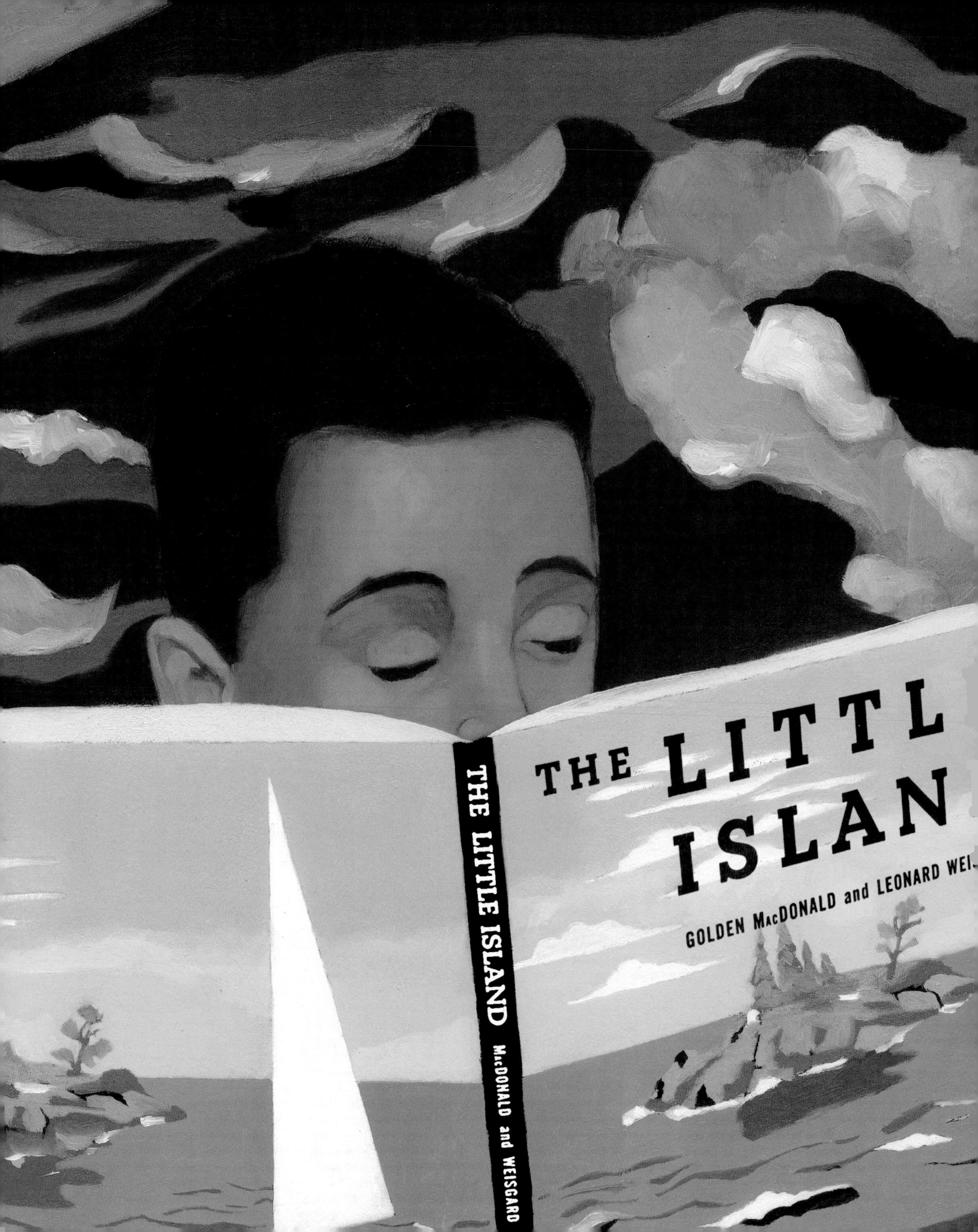
THE LITTL
ISLAN
GOLDEN MacDONALD and LEONARD WEI
THE LITTLE ISLAND
MacDONALD and WEISGARD

Then came the exciting part. I *knew* something exciting was going to happen. A great storm came to the island. I could almost hear the wind roaring and the waves crashing. But, wouldn't you know it, just as the story got exciting, the words got harder. Rats!

"Waves as big as glassy moun-tains came before it and light-ning and thunder and always the how-w-ling, moan-ing, whisss . . . tling, whistling wind."

I kept reading aloud. Miss Little's hand was on my shoulder now, and when I needed a little help, she gave it to me. Not much, just enough. She reminded me to "sound out" the words and to take my time.

We finally finished the book, and I knew all about a Little Island in a big ocean. Maybe I would even go there someday.

Miss Little gave me a hug, and I hugged her back.

"Very good, Douglas," she said. "I'm so proud of you!"

"Can we read another book tomorrow, Miss Little?" I asked.

"Why, Douglas, I wouldn't miss it for the world," she said with a smile. "Now don't forget your homework." She handed me a piece of paper with practice problems on it. Math! Ten times worse than reading. Rats!

The weeks went on, and we read many more books together as autumn turned into winter and winter into spring.

I didn't become a good reader right away, but I got better. And I didn't feel like jumping up from my desk and running outside quite so much.

Miss Little picked out books for me, books she thought I'd like, books to help me learn how much *fun* reading could be. Books to help me explore the world.

It was her gift to me — the gift of extra time and extra care, the gift of a wonderful teacher to a student who needed help. Mostly it was the gift of reading, the gift of books.

And many years later, when I understood the gift she'd given me, I sent a gift to Miss Little. It was a book — a book I'd written about a turtle.

Look, Miss Little, I wrote her. *I not only learned to read books — I even wrote one!* And I said thank you for her long-ago gift to me.

AUTHOR'S NOTE

As a child, I had a condition known as Attention Deficit Hyperactivity Disorder, or ADHD. And I still do.

This condition can make it hard to focus and keep your attention where it's supposed to be. It's easy to become distracted, to forget, or to have trouble following directions or sticking with something as difficult and complex as learning to read. It can seem impossible to sit still and "behave."

In those days, no one had heard of ADHD, but with the help and patience of Miss Little, other teachers, and my family, I learned how to cope and to succeed. I have now published twenty-five books for children and adults, plus half a dozen music albums, and have written for newspapers and magazines, and guided wilderness trips throughout the north woods of Minnesota and Canada. I am able to give speeches, readings, and performances all over the country.

I have also learned to make plenty of lists and check things off one at a time. I always have lots of projects to stay interested in. When I'm working, I get up from my desk frequently and love to walk and run and paddle a canoe and work in the woods. I still love to play sports and fish and just be outdoors.

I have understanding editors and a patient wife, who helps me with typing and using the computer and who knows not to send me to the grocery store without a list — and a reminder to *take* the list . . . and go to the *grocery* store. (I still have trouble "behaving.")

Nowadays doctors, teachers, and counselors know much more about ADHD and how to help people cope with it. Medications may even be carefully prescribed and taken, though I have chosen not to take any.

Scholars suggest that many creative and productive people throughout history may have had ADHD, including Leonardo da Vinci, Benjamin Franklin, Winston Churchill, Thomas Edison, and others.

The Little Island, written by Golden MacDonald (a pseudonym for Margaret Wise Brown) and illustrated by Leonard Weisgard, was published in 1946 by Doubleday. It won the Caldecott Medal. The book is still in print and available in paperback from Random House.

To the memory of Lois Little;
to my mother, Joyce; and to other
wonderful teachers everywhere
D. W.

To my fifth-grade teacher, Mr. Clow,
who encouraged storytelling and
drawing in his class and sparked my
interest in creating books
J. B.

Text copyright © 2009 by Douglas Wood
Illustrations copyright © 2009 by Jim Burke

First paperback edition 2017

The Little Island by Golden MacDonald and Leonard Weisgard (illustrator), copyright 1946 by Random House
Children's Books, a division of Random House, Inc. Used by permission of Doubleday, a division of Random House, Inc.

The Library of Congress has cataloged the hardcover edition as follows:

Wood, Douglas, date.
Miss Little's gift / Douglas Wood ; illustrated by Jim Burke.
p.   cm.
ISBN 978-0-7636-1686-1 (hardcover)
1. Hyperactive children — Education. 2. Reading (Elementary) 3. Attention-deficit-disordered children — Education.
4. Attention-deficit hyperactivity disorder.   I. Burke, Jim, ill. II. Title.
LC4713.4.W66 2009
371.94 — dc22   2008017915

ISBN 978-0-7636-9837-9 (paperback)

17 18 19 20 21 22 CCP 10 9 8 7 6 5 4 3 2 1

Printed in Shenzhen, Guangdong, China

This book was typeset in Bulmer.
The illustrations were created in oil on gessoed bristol board.

Candlewick Press
99 Dover Street
Somerville, Massachusetts 02144

visit us at www.candlewick.com